DATE DUE

ANKYLOSAURUS

Titles in the Dinosaur Profiles series include:

DINOSAUR PROFILES

ANKYLOSAURUS

Text by Fabio Marco Dalla Vecchia
Illustrations by Leonello Calvetti and Luca Massini

BLACKBIRCH PRESS
An imprint of Thomson Gale, a part of The Thomson Corporation

THOMSON
™
GALE

Detroit • New York • San Francisco • New Haven, Conn. • Waterville, Maine • London

Published in 2007 in North America by Blackbirch Press. Blackbirch Press is an imprint of Thomson Gale, a part of the Thomson Corporation.

Thomson is a trademark and Gale [and Blackbirch Press] are registered trademarks used herein under license.

For more information, contact
The Gale Group, Inc.
27500 Drake Rd.
Farmington Hills, MI 48331-3535
Or you can visit our Internet site at http://www.gale.com

Computer illustrations 3D and 2D: Leonello Calvetti and Luca Massini

Photographs: pages 20–21, Fabio Marco Dalla Vecchia

LIBRARY OF CONGRESS CATALOGING-IN-PUBLICATION DATA

Dalla Vecchia, Fabio Marco.
Ankylosaurus / text by Fabio Marco Dalla Vecchia ; illustrations by Leonello Calvetti and Luca Massini.
    p. cm.—(Dinosaur profiles)
Includes bibliographical references and index.
ISBN-13: 978-1-4103-0738-5 (hardcover)
ISBN-10: 1-4103-0738-7 (hardcover)
 1. Ankylosaurus—Juvenile literature. 2. Dinosaurs—Evolution—Juvenile literature.
 I. Calvetti, Leonello, ill. II. Massini, Luca, ill. III. Title.

QE862.O65D349 2007
567.915—dc22
                                                        2006103259

Printed in the United States of America
10 9 8 7 6 5 4 3 2 1

CONTENTS

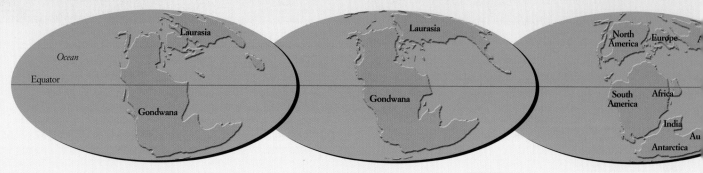

Late Triassic
228–206 million years ago

Early Jurassic
206–176 million years ago

Middle Jurassic
176–161 million years a

A Changing World

Earth's long history began 4.6 billion years ago. Dinosaurs are some of the most fascinating animals from the planet's long past.

The word *dinosaur* comes from the word *dinosauria*. This word was invented by the English scientist Richard Owen in 1842. It comes from two Greek words, *deinos* and *sauros*. Together, these words mean "terrifying lizard."

The dinosaur era, also called the Mesozoic era, lasted from 228 million years ago to 65 million years ago. It is divided into three periods. The first, the Triassic period, lasted 42 million years. The second, the Jurassic period, lasted 61 million years. The third, the Cretaceous period, lasted about 79 million years. Dinosaurs ruled the world for a huge time span of 160 million years.

Like dinosaurs, mammals appeared at the end of the Triassic period. During the time of dinosaurs, mammals were small animals the size of a mouse. Only after dinosaurs became extinct did mammals develop into the many forms that exist today. Humans never met Mesozoic dinosaurs. The dinosaurs were gone nearly 65 million years before humans appeared on Earth.

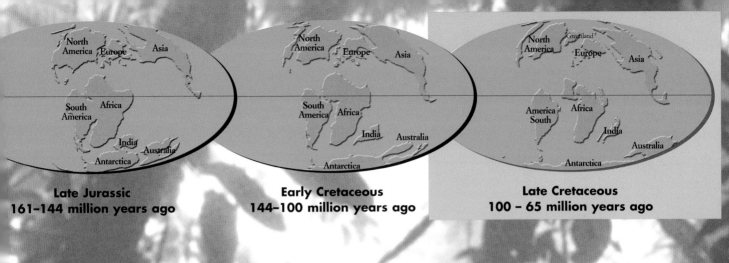

Late Jurassic
161–144 million years ago

Early Cretaceous
144–100 million years ago

Late Cretaceous
100 – 65 million years ago

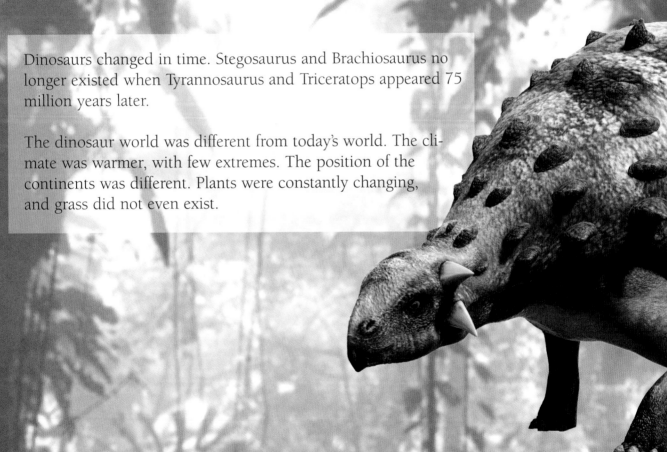

Dinosaurs changed in time. Stegosaurus and Brachiosaurus no longer existed when Tyrannosaurus and Triceratops appeared 75 million years later.

The dinosaur world was different from today's world. The climate was warmer, with few extremes. The position of the continents was different. Plants were constantly changing, and grass did not even exist.

An Armored Giant

Ankylosaurus was an enormous dinosaur whose body was covered in bony plates and spines. The name *Ankylosaurus* comes from Greek and means "lizard with joined bones." This name refers to the Ankylosaurus skull, which was a single block of connected bones.

Paleontologists (scientists who study dinosaurs) believe that Ankylosaurus weighed as much as 4 tons (3.6 metric tons). It was at least 20 feet (6m) long and perhaps as long as 33 feet (10m). It was quadrupedal, meaning it walked about on four legs. It had a large head, and its tail ended in a powerful structure that looked like a club. Despite its fearful appearance, however, Ankylosaurus probably ate only plants.

Ankylosaurus lived in North America at the end of the Late Cretaceous period, between 67 and 65.5 million years ago. It was related to the spiny Stegosauria of the Jurassic period. Remains of Ankylosaurus have been discovered in what are today Wyoming, Montana, and Alberta, Canada.

NORTH AMERICA

This map shows North America during the Late Cretaceous period. The brown areas show mountains. The red dots show places where Ankylosaurus fossils have been discovered.

9

Ankylosaurus Babies

No Ankylosaurus nests, eggs, or young have ever been found. But many remains of young Pinacosaurus, a relative of Ankylosaurus, have been discovered. Scientists who have examined these fossils believe a young Ankylosaurus probably was not armored like its parents. The bony plates might not have formed yet. The spines would have been nothing but bumps.

TEAR AND CHOP

Ankylosaurus mainly ate plants. The front part of its snout had no teeth. Instead, it had a beak that was used to tear food from trees. The mouth had around 35 teeth that were small, leaf-shaped, and jagged. Ankylosaurus used these teeth to chop up the leaves, buds, branches, and fruit that it ate.

PLANT EATERS EVERYWHERE

Ankylosaurus and its relatives lived in the same areas as horned dinosaurs such as Triceratops and hadrosaurs such as Edmontosaurus. These dinosaurs probably all gathered together at the edges of lakes when they came to drink water.

HITTING BACK

The only predator that was able to attack an animal as large as Ankylosaurus was Tyrannosaurus rex. Ankylosaurus probably moved slowly, so it could not easily run away from an attacker. But it was protected by the bony plates that covered its body and head. And it could use the club at the end of its tail for defense. With a swing of the powerful tail, Ankylosaurus could break the legs of any animal that threatened it.

THE ANKYLOSAURUS BODY

Ankylosaurus had a wide, triangle-shaped head. The head was completely covered with thick, bony plates. Two pairs of powerful spines or horns were located on the back part of the skull.

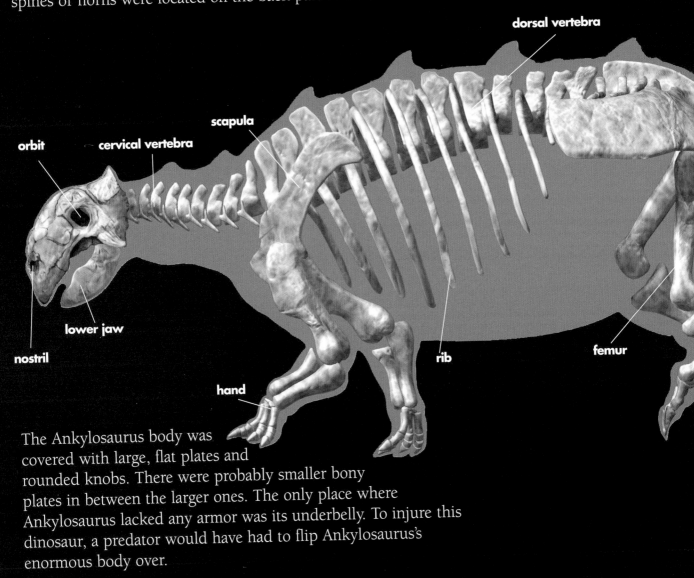

dorsal vertebra

scapula

orbit

cervical vertebra

lower jaw

nostril

hand

rib

femur

The Ankylosaurus body was covered with large, flat plates and rounded knobs. There were probably smaller bony plates in between the larger ones. The only place where Ankylosaurus lacked any armor was its underbelly. To injure this dinosaur, a predator would have had to flip Ankylosaurus's enormous body over.

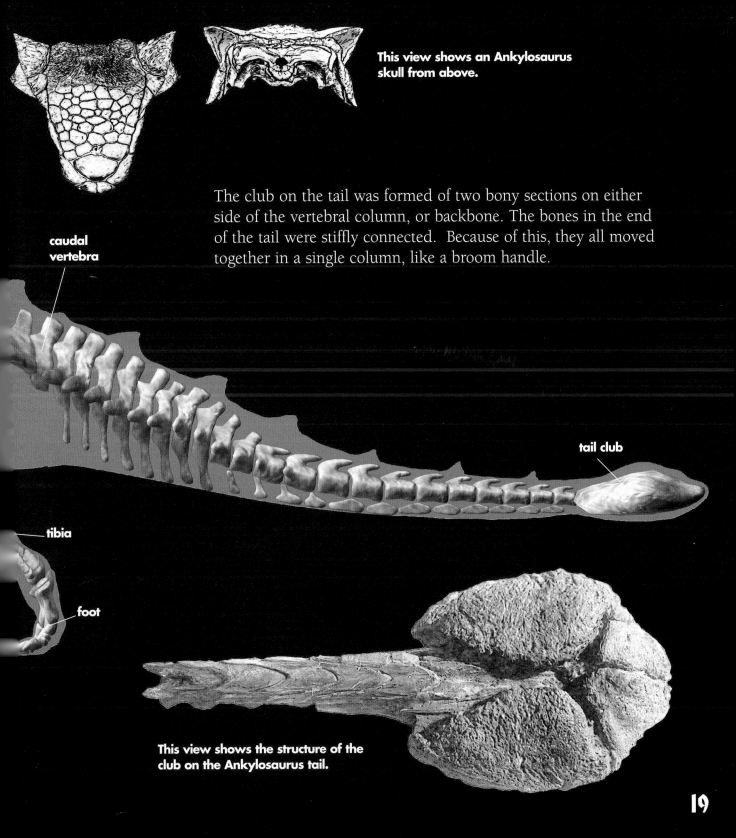

This view shows an Ankylosaurus skull from above.

caudal vertebra

The club on the tail was formed of two bony sections on either side of the vertebral column, or backbone. The bones in the end of the tail were stiffly connected. Because of this, they all moved together in a single column, like a broom handle.

tail club

tibia

foot

This view shows the structure of the club on the Ankylosaurus tail.

DIGGING UP ANKYLOSAURUS

The first Ankylosaurus parts were discovered by Peter Kaisen in 1906 in what is today Montana. He found pieces of a skull, parts of the armor and backbone, and rib bones. Two years later, the American paleontologist Barnum Brown gave the dinosaur the name Ankylosaurus. Brown at first thought that Ankylosaurus was a kind of stegosaur rather than an entirely different dinosaur.

Four years after Kaisen's find, more Ankylosaurus bones were found in Canada. These included a complete skull along with pieces of the armor and tail club. Most of the Ankylosaurus fossils that have been discovered so far are on display in the American Museum of Natural History in New York City.

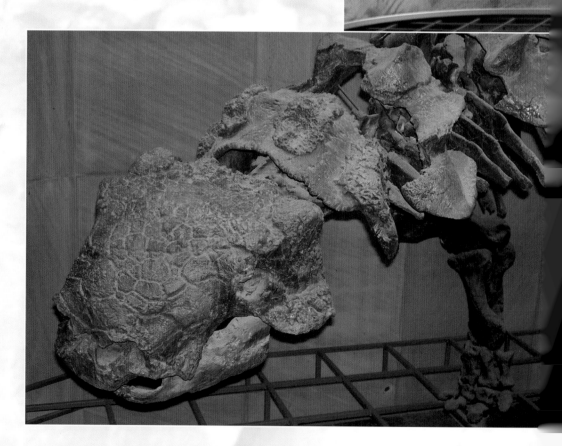

Above: This is a complete skeleton of Euoplocephalus, a close relative of Ankylosaurus. The club on the end of its tail can be seen clearly.

Left: This enormous skull of Euoplocephalus, like the skulls of all ankylosaurians, is covered with bony plates. Large plates also protected the neck.

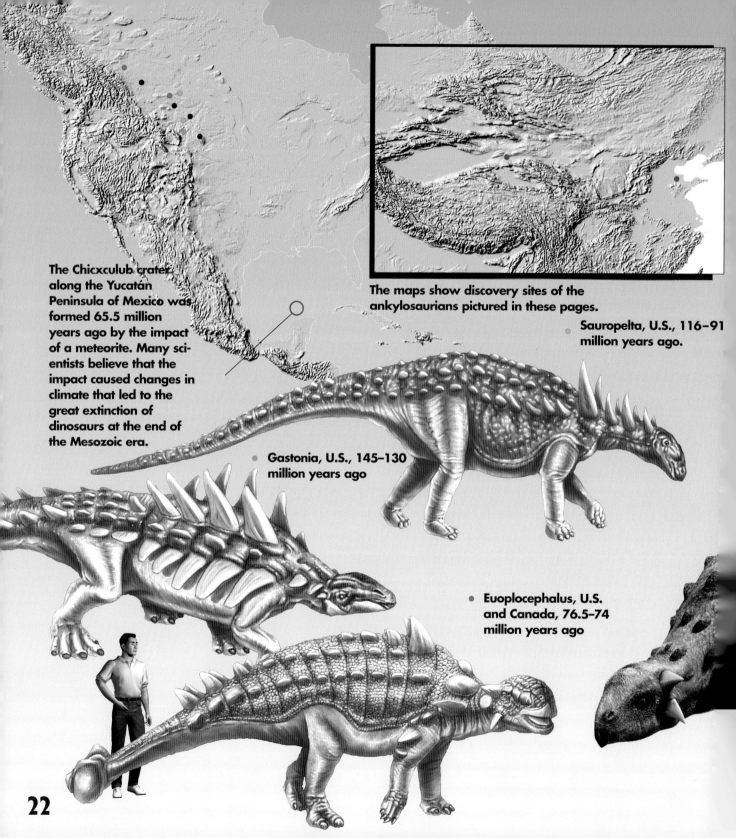

The Chicxculub crater along the Yucatán Peninsula of Mexico was formed 65.5 million years ago by the impact of a meteorite. Many scientists believe that the impact caused changes in climate that led to the great extinction of dinosaurs at the end of the Mesozoic era.

The maps show discovery sites of the ankylosaurians pictured in these pages.

Sauropelta, U.S., 116–91 million years ago.

Gastonia, U.S., 145–130 million years ago

Euoplocephalus, U.S. and Canada, 76.5–74 million years ago

ANKYLOSAURIANS

The ankylosaurians are divided into two groups. These are the Ankylosauridae, which had tail clubs, and the Nodosauridae, which did not. The Ankylosauridae lived mainly in what is today Asia. Only Ankylosaurus and Euoplocephalus lived in what is now North America.

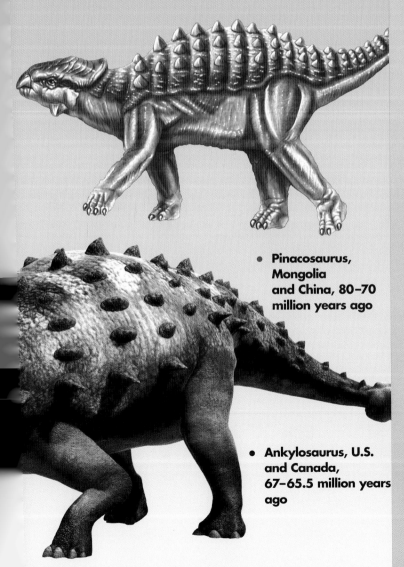

- **Pinacosaurus, Mongolia and China, 80–70 million years ago**

- **Ankylosaurus, U.S. and Canada, 67–65.5 million years ago**

THE GREAT EXTINCTION

Ankylosaurus was one of the last dinosaurs. Sixty-five million years ago, dinosaurs became extinct. This may have happened because a large meteorite struck Earth. A wide crater caused by a meteorite 65 million years ago has been located along the coast of the Yucatán Peninsula in Mexico. The impact of the meteorite would have produced an enormous amount of dust. This dust would have stayed suspended in the atmosphere and blocked sunlight for a long time. A lack of sunlight would have caused a drastic drop in Earth's temperature and killed plants. The plant-eating dinosaurs would have died, starved and frozen. As a result, meat-eating dinosaurs would have had no prey and would also have starved.

Some scientists believe dinosaurs did not die out completely. They think that birds were feathered dinosaurs that survived the great extinction. That would make the present-day chicken and all of its feathered relatives descendants of the large dinosaurs.

THE EVOLUTION OF DINOSAURS

The oldest dinosaur fossils are 220–225 million years old and have been found mainly in South America. They have also been found in Africa, India, and North America. Dinosaurs probably evolved from small and nimble bipedal reptiles like the Triassic Lagosuchus of Argentina. Dinosaurs were able to rule the world because their legs were held directly under the body, like those of modern mammals. This made them faster and less clumsy than other reptiles.

Since 1887, dinosaurs have been divided into two groups based on the structure of their hips. Saurischian dinosaurs had hips shaped like those of modern lizards. Ornithischian dinosaurs had hips shaped like those of modern birds.

Triceratops is one of the ornithischian dinosaurs, whose hip bones (inset) are shaped like those of modern birds.

Tyrannosaurus is in the saurischian group of dinosaurs, whose hip bones (inset) are shaped like those of modern lizards.

There are two main groups of saurischians. One group is sauropodomorphs. This group includes sauropods, such as Brachiosaurus. Sauropods ate plants and were quadrupedal, meaning they walked on four legs. The other group of saurischians, theropods, includes bipedal meat-eating predators. Some paleontologists believe birds are a branch of theropod dinosaurs.

Ornithischians are all plant eaters. They are divided into three groups. Thyreophorans include the quadrupedal stegosaurians, including Stegosaurus, and ankylosaurians, including Ankylosaurus. The other two groups are ornithopods, which includes Edmontosaurus and marginocephalians.

A DINOSAUR'S FAMILY TREE

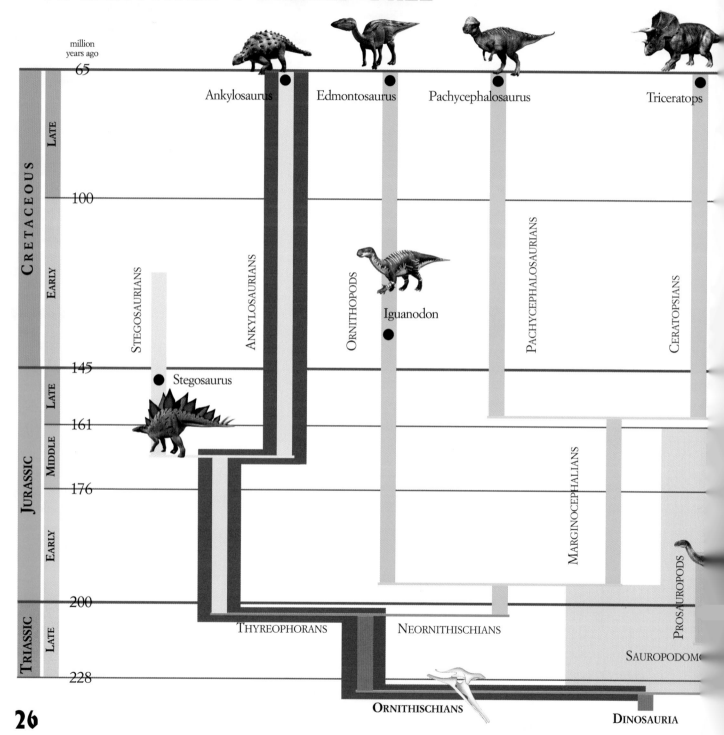

million years ago

CRETACEOUS

LATE

65

Ankylosaurus

Edmontosaurus

Pachycephalosaurus

Triceratops

100

EARLY

STEGOSAURIANS

ANKYLOSAURIANS

ORNITHOPODS

Iguanodon

PACHYCEPHALOSAURIANS

CERATOPSIANS

145

JURASSIC

LATE

Stegosaurus

161

MIDDLE

176

EARLY

MARGINOCEPHALIANS

PROSAUROPODS

200

TRIASSIC

LATE

THYREOPHORANS

NEORNITHISCHIANS

SAUROPODOMO

228

ORNITHISCHIANS

DINOSAURIA

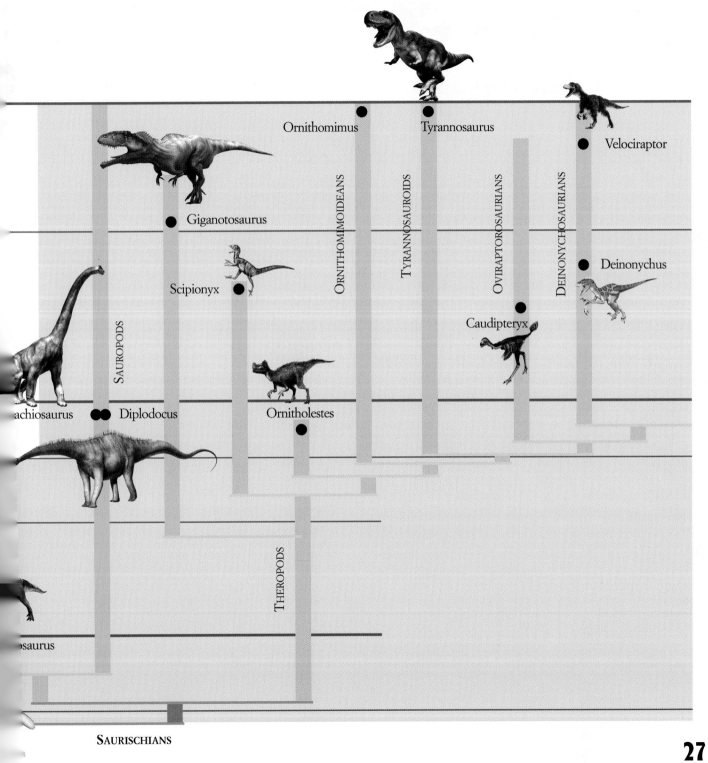

Ornithomimus

Tyrannosaurus

Velociraptor

ORNITHOMIMOIDEANS

TYRANNOSAUROIDS

OVIRAPTOROSAURIANS

DEINONYCHOSAURIANS

Giganotosaurus

Deinonychus

Scipionyx

SAUROPODS

Caudipteryx

Brachiosaurus • • Diplodocus

Ornitholestes

THEROPODS

...saurus

GLOSSARY

Bipedal moving on two feet

Caudal related to the tail

Cervical related to the neck

Cretaceous period the period of geological time between 144 and 65 million years ago

Dorsal related to the back

Evolution changes in living things over time

Femur thigh bone

Fossil part of a living thing, such as a skeleton or leaf imprint, that has been preserved in Earth's crust from an earlier geological age

Jurassic period the period of geological time between 206 and 144 million years ago

Mesozoic era the period of geological time between 228 and 65 million years ago

Meteorite a piece of iron or rock that falls to Earth from space

Paleontologist a scientist who studies prehistoric life

Predator an animal that hunts other animals for food

Prey an animal that is hunted by other animals for food

Quadrupedal moving on four feet

Skeleton the structure of an animal body, made up of bones

Skull the bones that form the head and face

Tibia shinbone

Triassic period the period of geological time between 248 and 206 million years ago

Vertebra a bone of the spine

Vertebral having to do with the bones of the spine

FOR MORE INFORMATION

Books

Daniel Cohen, *Ankylosaurus*. Mankato, MN: Capstone, 2006.

Douglas Dixon, *Ankylosaurus and Other Mountain Dinosaurs*. Bloomington, MN: Picture Window Books, 2004.

Virginia Schomp, *Ankylosaurus and Other Armored Plant-Eaters*. New York: Benchmark Books/Marshall Cavendish, 2003.

Web Sites

Dinosaur Hall
http://www.ansp.org/museum/dinohall/index.php
This section of the Web site of the Academy of Natural Sciences in Philadelphia contains a picture of a Giganotosaurus skull along with information about it and other dinosaurs, including Ankylosaurus.

Dinosaurs and Other Extinct Creatures
http://www.nhm.ac.uk/nature-online/life/dinosaurs-other-extinct-creatures/index.html
The Dino Directory section of this Web page created by London's Natural History Museum has information and many illustrations of Ankylosaurus's relative Euoplocephalus.

Walking with Dinosaurs
http://www.abc.net.au/dinosaurs/default.htm
The fact files section of this Web site contains information about many different dinosaurs, including Ankylosaurus.

About the Author

Fabio Marco Dalla Vecchia is the curator of the Paleontological Museum of Monfalcone in Gorizia, Italy. He has participated in several paleontological field works in Italy and other countries and has directed paleontological excavations in Italy. He is the author of more than 50 scientific articles that have been published in national and international journals.

Index

American Museum of Natural History
    (New York City), 20

ankylosaurians, 23, 25

Ankylosauridae, 23

babies, 11

bipedal dinosaurs, 25

birds, 23, 25

body, 8, 12, 17–19

Brachiosaurus, 7

Brown, Barnum, 20

climate, 7, 23

Cretaceous period, 6

dinosaurs, 6–7

evolution, 7, 23–24

extinction, 7, 23

food, 12

fossils, 20

head, 18

Jurassic period, 6

Kaisen, Peter, 20

living areas, 14

lizard with joined bones, 8

mammals, 6

marginocephalians, 25

Mesozoic era, 6

meteorite impact, 23

mouth, 12

movement, 8, 17, 24

name meanings, 6, 8

Nodosauridae, 23

Index